Banking on God

Exploring Salvation in the Bible

In our present age, the question "Are you saved?" sounds as quaint to many as "Mister, can you spare a dime?" It is a cliché from a bygone era. But for many Christians, the question of salvation is both relevant and a bit embarrassing. It is relevant because salvation lies at the heart of God's action as revealed in scripture. It is embarrassing because it has been trivialized and given an overly simplistic spin. If you are among those who have a certain perplexity about the Bible's notion of salvation and what its contemporary relevance is, you have come to the right place.

First, you will find in the following lessons that salvation in the Bible is a many splendored thing. It cannot be placed in a small box and still retain the many connotations it has in the Bible. Second, salvation will take on new meanings for you, meanings that are relevant and which I hope you can embrace and act on. Third, by the end of the present series, you should no longer be embarrassed when talking about salvation. Rather, you should be excited by its richness and relevance.

The following lessons follow a sequence that builds. You will begin with the deliverance of Israel at the Red Sea. The next lessons move to the New Testament and the teachings of Paul and the life and ministry of Jesus. At the end of the first four lessons, you should have an expanded and exciting new understanding of salvation as illustrated and described in the Bible. You should have meat into which you can sink your mental and spiritual teeth.

The final two lessons move to a more personal level, although the personal has not been absent in the first four. In these lessons you will consider how best to describe Christian experience and life. It is hoped you will end with a clearer understanding of what it means to be a Christian and how one lives in the world as a Christian.

Introduction

All this in six lessons! This is a pretty tall mission for such a short booklet. But the biblical material you will read, study, and discuss will stretch you and repay your commitment to it. In fact, groups have found that six sessions are not enough to cover the material as thoroughly as they would like. You may not want to be too rigid in allotting just one session for each lesson. If it seems fruitful, spend two sessions on some of them. Whatever time you have to give to reflection on God's saving grace in the world will make your faith more full.

About the Writer

Perry Yoder is a Bible scholar with a specialty in ancient Near Eastern studies and Semitic languages and literatures. Yoder is professor of Old Testament at Associated Mennonite Biblical Seminary in Elkhart, Indiana.

Welcome to Good Ground!

Now that you know a little about the topic for this unit, let us introduce you to Good Ground, the series. Good Ground is a unique approach to Bible study. It lets the Bible ask most of the questions and lets participants struggle with the answers. When we ask, "How can I be saved?" the Bible asks, "Whom will you serve?" When we ask, "What will happen to me when I die?" the Bible asks, "What does the Lord require of you?" When we ask, "Whom does God love best?" the Bible asks, "Who is your neighbor?" Good Ground goes to the Scriptures for questions, not just answers.

Here's how each session is structured and what you can expect:

Part I: Preparation

We assume that you want to dig into Bible texts enough to do a little reading and thinking between sessions. In this section you are given the Bible passage(s) for the session, a key verse, a summary of the text and the issues it raises, and a three-page study on the text. The section concludes with "Things to think about," which offers some practical applications for everyday living.

Introduction

We realize that in an age of prepackaged goods and 15-second sound bites, advance preparation may be a challenge. At the same time, we believe that for God's Word to be relevant to us, we need to do what it takes to ready our hearts and minds.

Part II: Session

Here we offer tips for your group when it meets, whether at church, in a home, or in some other setting. Good Ground uses a method for study that begins with everyday life (Focus), moves into an examination of what the Bible says (Engage the Text), then suggests life applications (Respond). The Closing wraps up the study in a brief worship experience.

One of the unique features about Good Ground studies is that they tap into a variety of learning styles. Some people learn best through the traditional lecture and discussion, but many others learn through visuals, imagination, poetry, role-playing, and the like. Through these varied learning experiences, Good Ground gets participants involved in the learning, moving beyond the head and into concrete living from the heart.

Part III: Leader Guidelines

We recognize that in many adult groups today, responsibility for leading is passed around within the group—hence the inclusion of notes for the leader in the participant's book. For these sessions to work best, however, those who lead must be prepared ahead of time. This section outlines what materials will be needed for the session, suggests some resources, and offers some tips for making the session come alive. If you are a regular leader of Good Ground, you will likely be aware of our other teaching/leading resources that orient you to our learning philosophy and methods.

Enjoy working with Good Ground as you journey in your faith, growing to be more like Christ!

>Julie Garber, editor
>Byron Rempel-Burkholder, editor
>Ken Hawkley, adult education consultant

Session 1
God Saves at the Red Sea Bank

Part I: Preparation

Bible Passage: Exodus 14:9-31

Key verse: But Moses said to the people, "Do not be afraid, stand firm, and see the deliverance that the LORD will accomplish for you today; for the Egyptians whom you see today you shall never see again. The LORD will fight for you, and you have only to keep still" (Exod. 14:13-14).

Summary: As Israel is fleeing Egypt, Pharaoh's army follows in hot pursuit to the banks of the Red Sea. Here, at the climax of the liberation of Israel, God alone saves Israel and drowns the enemy. This story of Israel's salvation at the sea has become the foundation of the Bible's witness to the God who saves. The curious thing about this story, however, is the character of the people God saves. Are they believers? the pure of heart? defenders of the faith? Why does God choose to save the undeserving? What does that mean for our own salvation?

Study

What excitement! Just a short time ago we were slaves building great buildings for Pharaoh. The work was hard, too hard for people to endure it long. Even worse, Pharaoh decreed that all of our male children were to be killed. We seemed doomed as a people. If it were not for sympathetic midwives, we would have been wiped out. But now God has finally heard our groans of agony and our cries of distress. God has intervened and brought judgment on the Egyptians for their stubborn cruelty. Who would have believed that we could ever have been delivered from such a powerful nation? But by God's action we were!

We celebrated God's deliverance with a new festival meal, the Passover. God commanded us to commemorate the night in which we were set free. It was a dreadful night, a night when God judged the Egyptians, causing their firstborn males to die, as had all of our tiny baby boys at the hands of Pharaoh. Now we were free and headed out into the desert to worship this God who had intervened on our behalf. Truly the Lord is a God who frees. How great it is to be alive and a member of God's people!

But, what is this? A cloud of dust. The sound of horses and chariots. The ground trembles with the galloping hooves of Egyptian horses. Is our freedom some kind of a cruel joke? Have we been brought out into the wilderness to be cut down like cattle? What worth is freedom to the dead? We should have stayed in Egypt. Living as a slave is better than being massacred in the wilderness.

The other side of the coin

It is an irony that God's great act of salvation for Israel was an act of judgment against the Egyptians. What's more, Israel's freedom from slavery came only after the deaths of their firstborn males. In Exodus 14, Israel's salvation comes only after the annihilation of the pursuing Egyptian army at the Red Sea. Apparently, salvation and mercy for some meant justice and punishment for others. But in the end, Israel was not saved because she was greater or more powerful than the Egyptians. She was not saved because of her great trust in God (14:31). Israel came to believe and have faith only *after* she had seen and experienced God's salvation. When Israel saw the Egyptian army amassing behind them, they cried out cynically, "Was it because there were no graves in Egypt that you have taken us away to die in the wilderness? . . . it would have been better for us to serve the Egyptians than to die in the wilderness" (14:11-12). What ingratitude! But then we, unlike them, aren't facing a certain and bloody death.

> God is a God who alone saves. There is no other.

In this dramatic context of certain death, Moses commands Israel to be still. She is not to act on her own behalf. It is God who will save her, in spite of her cold feet and ungratefulness. Here we find the first great fact about God's salvation: it is an unmerited miracle. Commit this sentence to memory as you begin your journey of understanding, "Stand still and see the salvation of the Lord."

This passage also reminds us that there are two sides to the shekel of salvation. On the one hand, the oppressed are liberated, but on the other

God Saves at the Red Sea Bank

hand, those who persist in oppression are brought low. Reflect this week on the relationship between salvation and judgment. How could the Egyptians have avoided judgment and participated in the saving activity of God toward Israel?

Things to think about: Think of a time when you were saved from death or physical injury. For example, have you been in an automobile accident in which you thought you would certainly be badly injured if not killed? What do you feel was God's role in this event? In what sense was this an act of salvation?

Part II: Session

Focus (10 minutes)

Open the session with announcements and sharing. Then choose one of the following options to focus on the topic of the session.

> Salvation, like apple pie baking in an oven, can be savored in process and enjoyed when done, if we can trust.

Option A: Take turns quickly telling about your nearest brush with death. Talk generally about whether you think your survival was luck or providence? What makes you think so?

Option B: Divide into pairs and as a team write down as many short definitions as you can for the word *save* (for example, "Bill *saves* stamps," "We packed everything *save* the kitchen sink," "He *saved* my life."). Then share your team definitions with the larger group. Work together as a large group to find a synonym for *save* in each case. What synonyms can you think of for *salvation*?

Option C: Play Oobat. Divide into several groups. As a small group, fill in the blank in this sentence: Stand still and see the _____ of the Lord. Limit yourselves to two minutes. Think of as many words as you can in the time allotted. When time is up, take turns reporting the first word on each group's list to a recorder who will write the words on a chalkboard or newsprint. In the next round, report your second word; in the third round, report your third word, and so on. When a group is out of words, it is eliminated from the game. When one group is left, the game is finished. As a whole group, look at the list of words. Judging from this list of words, how would you describe God? Merciful? Judging? Mysterious?

Engage the Text (20 MINUTES)

Option A: What does Exodus 14:9-31 say about action and inaction in the name of God who saves? Listen as a volunteer reads through Exodus 14:9-31. Then divide into three groups. Group 1 will examine the Israelites. Group 2 will examine the Egyptian army, and Group 3 will look at Moses. Use the following instructions to guide discussion in your group:

Group 1: When is inaction in the face of death the right thing to do?
Group 2: What happens when people take things into their own hands?
Group 3: How do we know we should do what God asks us to do?

Come back together as a large group and summarize your discussion for the other groups. God alone acts to save the Israelites in this story. Why do you suppose God saves these people? Is there any sense in which the Israelites participate in their own salvation? The Egyptians who oppress the Hebrews are judged in the end. If for some unknown reason God saves the undeserving, will God also save oppressors? Why or why not?

Option B: Listen as a volunteer reads Exodus 14:9-31 aloud. Together compare the disbelief of Israel expressed in verses 10-12 with Israel's belief in verse 31. How does the faith of the people figure into salvation in this story? What do you make of your findings?

Option C: Talk about Jesus and salvation. In small groups or individually, use concordances to look for the verse in the Bible that says "Jesus saves." What do you find? What does it mean to you when Jesus is called the Savior? Does Jesus succeed in saving the poor and oppressed he has come to save? Does he liberate them? What difference is there, if any, between saving the people and liberating them? Which are you? Why? Review the events of Jesus' persecution, sentencing, death, and resurrection. Remember, it was Passover time when Jesus was crucified. How would the early church have interpreted Jesus' death in light of the exodus from Egypt celebrated at Passover time?

Respond (20 MINUTES)

Option A: If you're willing, tell whether you believe you are saved and what that means to you. Break into small groups if you'd rather talk about your personal faith with just a few people. Also talk about how your understanding of salvation differs from the understanding of salvation in Exodus where the salvation of a whole people (stubborn ones at that) at the Red Sea is the model of God's saving action.

Option B: Practice being still. In Exodus 14 the people were commanded to be still and witness the salvation of God. That must have been very hard under the circumstances. Think about it—here was this massive army drawn up against them and no place to run! Can we stand still and witness the miracle of God's salvation in the following situations? Why or why not?

- Aging and declining health
- Retirement without a pension
- Terminal illness
- Debilitating condition or injury
- Broken relationship
- Social injustice

Work together to define what trust in a saving God looks like. How would you live your life? For instance, would you buy insurance? Would you join volunteer service? Would you practice preventive medicine?

Closing (5 MINUTES)

Stand in a circle. Be silent for a full minute or more. In silence pray for the saving acts of God in the world today. If you feel led, pray for a situation in your life or in the world where God's salvation is needed. Close by singing "Go down Moses" or another song of God's salvation.

PART III: LEADER GUIDELINES

Resources
Perry B. Yoder. *Shalom: The Bible's Word for Salvation, Justice and Peace.* Nappanee, Ind.: Evangel Publishing House, 1987.

Tips for Leading
1. As a leader or facilitator, encourage group-building. To help the group feel like a community, begin each session with time for announcements and sharing.
2. Review all exercises you plan to do, and gather the items you will need. In Focus consider asking one person to tell a dramatic story of survival and build discussion around one event instead of many. Let the person relate the experience and how it has affected his or her life.
3. Gauge whether the group prefers to work in small, intimate groups or whether the large group is better for discussion. Engage everyone in

conversation. Ask those who make frequent contributions to wait until others have had a chance to speak.
4. This introductory session focuses on God's saving acts. Keep the group from wandering off in their conversation to talk about other aspects of salvation, such as the spiritual nature of salvation. These topic will come up in subsequent sessions.

Session 2
God Loves You All

PART I: PREPARATION

Bible Passage: Romans 5:1-11

Key verse: But God proves his love for us in that while we still were sinners Christ died for us (Rom. 5:8).

Summary: Paul describes Christ's death in Romans 5 as an act of love. Before the death of Christ, we were, as verse 6 says, "weak" and "ungodly." That Christ died even for us sinners tells us that his death is a sign of God's love for us. Paul uses three words to describe the effect of Christ's death upon us: *reconciliation*, *justification*, and *salvation*. While in this passage the first two are present realities, the third is future. What does that mean for our security? What does it mean for our lives?

Study

As you study this passage, focus on what Christ's death means for you in the present. Last week we saw that God's salvation had a real and present impact on the lives of the Israelites. The question now is, What real and present impact does the death of Christ have on our lives?

To help answer this question, examine the words *justified*, *reconciled*, and *saved* more closely. Note that, at first, Paul points out we are "justified" by Christ's blood. *Justified* is a legal term and means that one is declared to be just, or innocent, as in a court of law when a defendant is declared innocent. In this passage Paul claims we are now declared innocent by God.

Second, Paul couples justification with salvation. We who are now justified will also be saved from "the wrath" (5:9, English translators have added "of God"). To emphasize this linkage, Paul repeats it in verse 10, but this time he uses the word *reconciliation*. If we are reconciled to God by Christ's death, how much more shall we be saved by his life. Reconciliation describes a relationship. We, who were once related to God as enemies, now have a positive relationship with God. Not only are we innocent, we are on good terms with God.

Third, Paul declares, "We *shall* be saved." Note the future tense. In fact, every time Paul uses the Greek word here translated "save" (*sodzo*) in the book of Romans, he places it in the future tense (Rom. 5:9, 10; 8:24; 9:27; 10:9,13; 11:14, 26). Indeed, normally Paul uses *save* in the future tense, although translators may gloss over this fact by translating it as present, or even as past.

Let's be clear about what Paul claims. On the one hand, we are justified and reconciled *now*. This is our present experience. Note Paul's use of the word *now* in this passage as he stresses that justification and reconciliation are in the present.

This passage broadens our understanding of Jesus as Savior. He is also Reconciler and Justifier in addition to the one who saves us "from wrath." Driving down a road outside of Ely, Minnesota, I saw a billboard that asked the question: "Is Christ Your Personal Savior"? In light of this passage, that question strikes me a little odd. At first it looked like they meant "Is Christ your personal valet?" Then I wondered why they didn't ask a more biblical question, such as, "Are you reconciled with God?" or "Will you be saved?"

> Paul speaks of love as the reason Christ died for us. Christ's death is the proof that God loves us, all of us, regardless of who we are or what we have done. Yet we must ask ourselves, How does Christ's death, which happened 2,000 years ago, express love for me today?

As in the Exodus story, salvation is not something we can call on personally when we're in a pinch. Salvation is God's miraculous action over which we have no control. And according to Paul, it is something that is in the future. We can, however, embrace the justification God grants and live as people reconciled to God. That is miraculous enough—that we, while still sinners, are found innocent and invited into the arms of God. What does it mean, then, to live as people who are reconciled to God? Our challenge, one we do have control over, is to live faithfully and to trust that our salvation is in the hands of God, who has already proven great love for us.

Things to think about: Use a concordance to look for the phrase "personal Savior" in the Bible. What biblical basis is there for using the term "personal Savior"? Is this term for Christ a contrast with an "impersonal Savior"?

God Loves You All

Doctrines of the atonement explain how it is that Christ's death "saves" us. Some have said that Jesus was an example to instruct us and call us to godly living. Others have said Jesus died so that there would be one person, who is perfect, who would die for the rest of us, who are not perfect. Still others have said that humankind was in bondage to the devil, and in order to free them, God struck a deal with the devil. The God-Man was the ransom that the devil took to free humanity.

Try asking friends and family members at work, school, or home if they've been "reconciled" instead of saved. Then talk together about what that means. How does each of you feel about your relationship to God? What could each of you do to improve your relationship with God?

Part II: Session

Focus (10 minutes)

Gather for announcements and sharing. Then choose one of the following exercises to focus on the passage.

Option A: Have a discussion. Ask yourselves the provocative question, What did Christ's death really accomplish? Quickly look through Romans 5:6-11 for the several benefits listed there. What others would you add? Don't forget benefits like the founding of the church.

Option B: Answer the street preacher's questions. Take turns quickly answering three questions with one- or two-word answers:
1. Are you saved?
2. Are you justified (found not guilty)?
3. Are you reconciled to God?

Then discuss these questions generally as a group. Expand on your brief answers, if you wish. Talk about which question is most important for your life right now. Which question is most difficult for you? Why?

Option C: Role play the part of a missionary. Suppose you are working with a group of people who have never heard of Jesus. How would you describe salvation to them on the basis of Romans 5:6-11?

Engage the Text (20 minutes)

Option A: Take a broader look at Paul's view of salvation and the meaning of Christ's death. If you are a large group, divide into small groups to discuss the following questions.
1. Listen as someone reads Romans 5:6-11 aloud. How do you think

Christ's death accomplished justification and reconciliation? How will it provide salvation in the future? Will we know if we are going to be saved? How can we know for sure? Why is God determined to save us even though we are "ungodly"?
2. Listen as someone reads Galatians 2:21. As in Romans, *justification* is a key word for Paul. Why do you think Paul downplays justification that comes by following religious law? Why should we or shouldn't we be obedient to biblical laws like the Ten Commandments? Won't obedience make our case before God better? How do the notions of justification and salvation relate?
3. Now read 2 Corinthians 5:14-21 and its description of how Christians are transformed and given a mission. Then talk about how you would describe the relationship between reconciliation and salvation? How did Christ's death reconcile people to God?

Option B: Compare God's salvation of Israel at the Red Sea with God's salvation in Christ as described by Paul. Talk about how of each of the following terms figures into the story of the exodus and the story of Jesus' death.

oppression
blood
Passover
love
faithfulness (God's and the people's)
justification
reconciliation
salvation

Now that you've compared the stories, how are they different? How is Moses different from Jesus? Which one is a story of physical salvation, and which is a story of spiritual salvation? In what ways do you expect salvation to be physical? In what ways is salvation spiritual?

Respond (20 MINUTES)
Option A: Make a devotional response to Paul's description of salvation. In Romans 5:6-11, the terms *reconciliation* and *love* are very important. Write a brief note to God. Give thanks for being able to be a friend, rather than an enemy, of God. Also thank God for being a God who loves us even though there are no compelling reasons to do so.

Also tell God how you are responding to this love. How has God's love in Christ shaped you and your life? How does your friendship with God take expression in your life? How is your life an offering of thanks to the God who loves you and who died for you?

Let this letter be a reminder to you that God loves you.

Option B: Go back to the questions you discussed in the Focus exercise. Tell how you would respond to someone who asks you, "Are you reconciled?" "Are you justified?" "Will you be saved?"

Option C: Brainstorm a ministry of reconciliation. Surely God expects us to live as people who are found not guilty and who are reconciled to God. 2 Corinthians 5 actually gives the faithful the ministry of reconciliation to do. What would you say is involved in a ministry of reconciliation? Is your congregation involved in such a ministry? Are you personally? In what way? What would it take to put a ministry of reconciliation into action?

Option D: Put together a tract. Work together or in small groups to rough out a tract titled "Will You Be Saved?" How would you tell someone in very simple language about salvation as Paul has described it? If you like the pamphlet that comes together, consider putting it into print for distribution. Hand it out to members of the congregation first, then to others in the community. Be sure to include information about your congregation, particularly a schedule for worship and Bible study.

Closing (5 MINUTES)
Gather in a circle and pray a prayer of confession and thanksgiving. Offer sentence prayers confessing what Paul calls "ungodliness"; then pray sentence prayers of thanksgiving for God's unending love despite our ungodliness. Close with a hymn of God's love, such as "Come, let us all unite to sing" or "Love divine, all loves excelling."

PART III: LEADER GUIDELINES

Tips for Leading
1. This lesson is about more abstract and spiritual matters. Two key notions in this lesson are that salvation, according to this passage, is future, and love is the reason for God's saving action in Christ. Make sure these concepts come through.

2. Many people view atonement (God's act to save the people through Christ's death) in one way. Acknowledge that the New Testament uses a wide variety of metaphors for God's action. Avoid getting mired in debates about atonement. Focus on the reason for God's action and the immediate result as described by Paul—justification and reconciliation.
3. Keep making comparisons to the previous lesson, noting again and again that salvation is an act of God. We benefit from but we can't perform salvation.

Session 3

Trust and Salvation

Part I: Preparation

Bible Passage: Luke 18:9-27; 19:1-9

Key verses: Jesus looked at him and said, "How hard it is for those who have wealth to enter the kingdom of God! Indeed, it is easier for a camel to go through the eye of a needle than for someone who is rich to enter the kingdom of God." Those who heard it said, "Then who can be saved?" He replied, "What is impossible for mortals is possible for God" (Luke 18:24-27).

Summary: This cluster of parables and stories in Luke deals with salvation as the motivation for doing good. The Pharisee believes he is already saved and can therefore do no wrong. The ruler believes he cannot be saved because he cannot do the good thing Jesus asks of him. But Zacchaeus, who has nothing to gain from Jesus but condemnation, does the faithful thing and offers half his fortune to the poor, more than the law required for restitution. What motivates us to be good? The belief that we're already saved? The belief that our good deeds will be rewarded in the future? Or, like Zacchaeus, the love of God for God's sake, whatever the judgment may be on our lives? How can we get ourselves into that attitude?

Study

The Bible has already established in the story of the exodus from Egypt that salvation is one of God's miracles. Like a camel going through the eye of a needle, it is something we as humans cannot do for ourselves. Still, every generation wants to know what it can do "to inherit eternal life." Our text for this lesson contains some of Jesus' many responses to the age-old question, but we're never very satisfied with the answer we get. This passage contains some of the hardest sayings of Jesus, including "Sell all that you own and distribute the money to the poor, and you will have treasure in heaven" (Luke 18:22). It is not an ambiguous answer. Why is it so hard?

All along Jesus says it is not possible to buy salvation or bargain for eternal life. So why does it appear in this passage that the ruler can follow some simple rules and assure his place in heaven? Moreover, it seems like Jesus is being unfair. To require the rich man to sell everything is to require a greater price than a poor man has to pay. Of course, there are other inequities in Jesus' system. Obviously, not everyone was invited to follow after Jesus as his disciple, at least in a literal sense. Was the ruler to become Disciple 13? Probably not. Was Jesus addressing the particular situation of the ruler apart from the situations of all other people? Perhaps. But more than likely Jesus is making a general statement not about being saved, but about the difficulty of being faithful. He is judging our motivations for wanting to be saved.

> Trust is our disposition toward the God who saves. Trust is also our response to the experience of God's salvation. Obedience is its sign. We cannot serve both God and wealth. God or Gold.

A better way to understand this hard saying about giving up our wealth is to compare it to Jesus' answer to the same question in Luke 10:27-28. There, when the lawyer asks how he can be saved, the answer is to love God with all of one's being and to love your neighbor as yourself. This meant, to put it in the theological language of Jesus' day, that one needed to take upon oneself the yoke of the kingdom of God (total dedication to God alone) and the yoke of the commandments of God (to serve the neighbor). It is on these two commitments that our life hangs.

If we were to lay these stories side by side, we would understand why Jesus quizzes the ruler about keeping specific laws of the Ten Commandments. All the commandments Jesus mentions in the story of the rich ruler have to do with loving our fellow human beings. Now look at the narrative about the two men praying in the first part of the section. Notice the sinners mentioned by the Pharisee. They are the ones who have broken the commandments governing the way we treat neighbors. So how does the rich ruler rate on the requirements to love God and love his neighbor? How does divesting of his wealth and giving it to the poor and following Jesus show that he has taken up both the yoke of heaven and the yoke of the neighbor?

Just as the Israelites at the Red Sea had to trust God with their lives, so also Jesus is calling for the rich man to trust God rather than the security of his wealth. But he cannot. The opposite happens when Zacchaeus divests his wealth, indicating his willingness to trust in God, even though he knows he deserves condemnation for being a tax collector, a dishonest one at that. This trust was a sign of his willingness to depend on God rather than on his own substance. And by divesting he also cares for the well-being of his neighbors.

The stories of the rich ruler and Zacchaeus lead us to the question we must ask ourselves: Regardless of the state of our mortal souls, do we act out of our trust in God or out of the security we find in our wealth? I think I saw the answer to this question in an image that was repeated over and over as I traveled down the road one time. I was struck by how many farms I saw on the prairie with two houses. In each case, the older, smaller house was the original home, now the residence of the parents or grandparents. The other house was a larger, more modern home for the second generation of the family. These homesteads were graphic reminders for me of how our standard of living has risen dramatically since World War II. And it is a graphic reminder of our increasing dependence on wealth to sustain us instead of our trust in God.

When is enough enough? It is said we live in a material age in a materialistic society. We as Christians have prospered along with our fellow North Americans. Where do I draw the line? When do I decide to live on just enough and give the rest to the poor? It isn't a trivial question or an overly pious one. The gap between rich and poor in North America is increasing. From the middle 1980s to the middle 1990s, there was a significant shift in wealth to the wealthiest families in North America. The percentage of all available wealth going to the rich increased more than twofold. This has meant less for many, many others. In a democratic society, how do we exercise our citizenship so that the poor are not excluded from our general prosperity?

So, will care for our neighbors *and* trust in God get us a front row seat in eternity? We don't know. Zacchaeus didn't know. He put his trust in God and gave away his fortune without knowing how God would judge him. He was motivated out of great love for a loving God. Only later did Jesus say, "Today salvation has come to this house" (19:9). May we, like Zacchaeus, act out of trust and love for God and neighbor, leaving our salvation to God.

Things to think about: When you sit down to pay bills this month, think about whether you could reduce your expenses by half. What expenses would you get rid of? What would you do with the money you save? Consider making a gift to an organization that helps the poor. Decide together as a family where you will give the money.

Also talk with others this week about whether God wants people to prosper. How much prosperity is enough?

Part II: Session

Gather to share announcements and concerns. Then choose one of the following exercises to focus on the session.

Focus (10 minutes)

Option A: Look through real estate ads in the weekend newspaper. Find a dream house, a house you would love to own if you had the money. Then find a house at half the value of the house you live in or an apartment at half the rent you are currently paying. Share the picture or description of the house with others in the group. Tell whether you would be willing to live in the less expensive house.

Option B: Register your opinion on eternal life. Form a human continuum, standing at one side of the room if you believe that Christians who lead an exemplary life will be saved. Stand at the other end if you feel you are already saved, which causes you to lead an exemplary life. If you are somewhere between these extremes, find a place on the imaginary line between them. Take turns telling why you are standing where you're standing.

Option C: Take turns describing for each other what you think eternal life is. Feel free to draw your image of eternal life to share with others. What makes eternal life attractive to you? At this point in your study, do you think eternal life and salvation are the same?

Transition: The promise of eternal life has been a great motivating force in people's lives for thousands of years. If we live the good life, it stands to reason, we'll be rewarded. In Jesus' parables and stories, however, he warns against believing that we can work out our salvation by doing good deeds. Jesus uses the story of Zacchaeus to help us understand the true relationship between being good and the miracle of salvation.

Trust and Salvation

Engage the Text (20 MINUTES)

Option A: Listen as readers read or dramatize the stories of the Pharisee, the rich young ruler, and Zacchaeus. Then use this exercise to carefully compare the story of the rich young ruler (Luke 18:18-27) and the story of Zacchaeus (Luke 19:1-9). To help see the similarities and differences, take a piece of paper and divide it into two columns. Label one THE RICH MAN and the other THE TAX COLLECTOR. To the left of the columns, write these words: WEALTH, COMMANDMENTS, TRUST IN GOD, THE POOR, SALVATION. In each column tell what attitude the two characters had to the term on the left.

When everyone has had time to fill out the chart, take turns sharing the responses on your chart with the group. Talk together in general about the relationship between love of God, doing good works, and salvation. What does the rich ruler do wrong? What does Zacchaeus do right?

Option B: Regardless of whether or not we are saved, Jesus asks the faithful to love God and neighbor. This is not a new concept in the New Testament. Turn to the Ten Commandments in Exodus 20:1-17. Then turn to the Great Commandment in Luke 10:27-28. On a chalkboard or newsprint, make two columns. Call one LOVE OF GOD and the other LOVE OF NEIGHBOR. Arrange each of the Ten Commandments in the appropriate column. Place the commandments having to do with the way we relate to God in the LOVE OF GOD column, and place the commandments having to do with the way we relate to neighbors in the LOVE OF NEIGHBOR column. Then discuss whether the characters in the parables and stories of Luke 18–19 have fulfilled all that is required of them. Also talk about why they should fulfill the Great Commandment if they are not guaranteed salvation by doing so.

Respond (20 MINUTES)

Option A: Practice trust. As the rich young ruler learned, it is essential to trust God in order to experience reconciliation. The ruler went away sad because he could not trust. How much do you trust God? Talk together about the following questions. At the end, judge whether you are, as a group, trusting of God.

1. Would you be willing to give up at least half of your wealth to help others?
2. Would you be willing to take a job serving God in some way, such as working with the poor, caring for the elderly, or ministering with youth and children?
3. Would you be willing to break the law for a matter of conscience?

4. Would you be willing to forego life insurance or health insurance?
5. Would you be willing to associate with "sinners," such as felons, adulterers, non-Christians?
6. Would you be willing to take the risk of following Jesus simply out of love and without the promise of rescue or salvation?

Option B: In the last session, we found that justification and reconciliation with God are gifts of God we presently enjoy. We also saw that our reconciliation is the foundation for our trust in God and our future salvation from judgment. How, if at all, does each character in the passages for this session demonstrate he is reconciled with God? For those who are reconciled, how great is their trust?

Break into pairs or groups of three. Talk with your partners about the degree of reconciliation and trust you feel with God. Talk together about what you could do to increase the level of reconciliation and trust. Come back together as a large group and offer up the best suggestions from your small group for increasing reconciliation and trust.

Option C: Jot down a list of things that make you feel secure. Now prepare a parallel list of what makes you feel insecure. Look at the two lists and imagine you were to give up one of your "security blankets." How would this affect your feeling of security? Would this place you in jeopardy? Resolve to continue to think about your life in the light of your trust in God's salvation.

At the bottom of your list, write down the Lord's Prayer. As a group, talk about how the Lord's Prayer emphasizes the themes of trust, reconciliation, salvation, and good works, which have been the major themes of this study so far.

Closing (5 MINUTES)
Pray the Lord's Prayer three times, noting each time its emphasis on trusting in God to act and its call to us to live as disciples.

PART III: LEADER GUIDELINES

Tips for Leading
1. Focus on two questions presented by the stories in this session: Do we do good things because we expect a reward? Do we fail to do the right

things because our security is at stake? Encourage discussion at a deeper level on whether we love God because of what we hope to gain or do we love God for God's own self.
2. Bring a weekend paper to the session. Use the real estate advertisements in the Focus activity. If you use the continuum exercise in the Focus section, take time to debrief on why everyone arranged themselves as they did and what they think of others who took a different position.
3. Use care to avoid judging people for the good things they do or don't do. Try to challenge participants without condemning them. When talking about difficult issues, be the first one to admit your own weaknesses, opening the way for others to examine themselves without judgment.

Session 4
Your Faith Has Made You Well

Part I: Preparation

Bible Passage: Mark 5:21-43

Key verses: Then one of the leaders of the synagogue named Jairus came and, when he saw him, fell at his feet and begged him repeatedly, "My little daughter is at the point of death. Come and lay your hands on her, so that she may be made well, and live" (Mark 5:22-23).

Summary: In this passage, two people ask for salvation from Jesus. One is a father who asks Jesus to spare the life of his young daughter who is on the brink of death. The other is the woman who suffered from hemorrhages for twelve years. While he attends to the older woman, saving her from her affliction, reports come that the young girl has died. Jesus intervenes to save the girl and revitalize her. What does Mark mean by salvation in this sense? When we're saved from a crippling or fatal physical condition, is it the same as being saved for eternal life? Is there only one type of salvation?

Study

The text for this session is a "Markan sandwich." That is, it begins and ends with one set of actors, but in the middle of this story, another story takes place. The "outside" narrative about Jairus's daughter, which begins and ends the passage, is like sandwich bread. The "inside" story of the woman with a hemorrhage is like sandwich filling. Together all the fixings, bread and filling, are what make a sandwich a sandwich. Likewise, both the outer and the inner stories in this passage make it a single story of salvation.

Your Faith Has Made You Well

In both of these stories, Jesus "saves" individuals from physical ailments. In other instances, he talks about salvation as eternal life. So when we say that familiar slogan "Jesus Saves," what do we really mean? How did the people of Jesus' time experience his saving activity during his ministry?

The notion of salvation is getting complicated. Exodus talks about God's miraculous act to save an entire people. In Session 2, Paul talked about salvation as an event in the future, one that hasn't really been accomplished yet. Then in Session 3, Jesus considers the question "What must I do to inherit eternal life?" This question also addresses the future. Eternal life is a life everlasting beyond the physical life in the present. But the passage for this session focuses on the people around Jesus in the present who ask for salvation in a very different way from the rich young ruler. They want to be saved from torturous and deadly physical conditions. How then does Jesus truly save people?

> Those who are well have no need of a physician.

English translations take a certain amount of liberty with the Greek text, especially when it comes to the word "save," which is *sodzo* in Greek. Jairus asks Jesus literally, "Come and lay your hands on her, so she may be saved and live." When he uses the word *sodzo* here, he is not asking for eternal life. He is asking Jesus to save his daughter's physical life so that she will not die from her present ailment.

Later on, in the middle story, the woman thinks to herself, "If only I can touch his garment, I will be *saved*!" (v. 28). She wants deliverance from her disease, but says nothing of eternal life. In the next verse she touches Jesus' garment and is healed. In Jesus' response to her, he says, "Your faith has *saved* you, go in peace, be healed of your disease." Here again the word *save* and the word *heal* occur in parallel. While salvation is a gift from God that cannot be earned, there is some sense in these stories that we participate with God in healing and salvation. At the very least, we seek reconciliation with God by coming to God and offering our faith and devotion to the one who saves. Perhaps faith and reconciliation are salves that heal.

These stories are not unique in the ministry of Jesus. Examine other passages in Mark where the word *sodzo* appears (Mark 3:4; 6:56; 10:52; 15:30-31). *Sodzo* or salvation is translated several ways: to be made well, to be healed, and to be saved from an affliction. If you were to judge from this use of the word *salvation*, how would you describe the saving actions of Jesus in the New Testament?

While Mark shows us a different meaning of salvation, he also picks up on themes we saw in Exodus. Notice, for instance, how Jesus' healing ministry is similar to the way God saved Israel at the Red Sea. In both cases actual physical life is at stake. In both cases deliverance is deliverance from a physical threat. In both cases salvation is something that happens now and involves the physical dimension. Can God's salvation of Israel and Jesus' saving actions in Mark be connected in some way with eternal life or spiritual salvation? The greatest question Mark raises, however, is whether physical salvation and spiritual salvation be separated?

If the church only offers people a future life, it offers them no life at all.

Things to think about: Answer these questions for yourself or ask others how they would answer.
1. What would you like to be saved from?
2. What physical conditions or elements disable you or others you know?
3. In what sense could you be saved from your condition? Recovery? Acceptance?
4. How do you think your life would change if God saved you from a terminal illness and gave you more years to live?

PART II: SESSION

Focus (15 MINUTES)
Gather for sharing, announcements, and introductions. Then choose one of the following options to focus on the topic.

Option A: Do a matching exercise. On your own quickly match the word in the left column with its opposite in the right column.

1. already   A. training
2. reality   B. safety
3. body   C. dream
4. instinct   D. soul
5. independence   E. knowledge
6. faith   F. not yet
7. danger   G. reliance

Key: 1-F, 2-C, 3-D, 4-A, 5-G, 6-E, 7-B

Compare your answers with others in the group. Imagine that each pair is two sides of one coin. How do the two terms relate? In other words, how can both terms operate at the same time in one situation or one person?

Transition: On one hand, salvation is a present event. On the other, it is a future event. On one hand, salvation is God's miracle alone. On the other hand, salvation happens in our relationship with God. On one hand, salvation refers to the eternal salvation of the soul, but in the stories of Jesus in Mark, salvation is the salvation of the physical body. Study the text together to see how salvation can be all these things at once.

> Compassion is a response to present need. Jesus' compassion met people at their point of need, be it feeding, be it healing, or even, be it wine for rejoicing.

Option B: Make a pie chart. Individually or as a group, draw a circle on newsprint or a chalkboard to represent the congregation's budget. Come to an agreement as a group over what percentage of the budget will go to evangelism and how much will go to outreach services, such as feeding the poor, or cleaning up after natural disasters. Remember you must all agree. Where does the group come out? Where do you come out personally? Talk about whether these two budget items can be separated. In what sense is evangelism also a type of service? In what sense is service a type of evangelism? Would you change the percentages for budget expenditures following this discussion? How?

Transition: The Bible speaks of salvation in different ways, but all ways are related. What is good for the body is good for the soul. What is good for the soul is good for the body. What is future is also present. It's not necessary to choose one over the other, as Jairus's daughter and the woman with a hemorrhage can testify.

Engage the Text (15 MINUTES)

Option A: Read today's passage and mark the three times the word *sodzo* (to save) appears in the text. Also mark the other places in Mark where the word *sodzo* is used (see references in the study). Now go back as a group and look at each one. What happens in each case? Normally, in Jesus' ministry as recorded in the Gospels, salvation is a physical salvation, as in this passage. How do you think physical salvation is connected to spiritual salvation in these passages? Also discuss the differences you see in the two cases of physical healing—Jairus's daughter and the woman with the hemorrhage? Why do you think Mark puts these two stories together in a "sandwich"?

Option B: Divide into two groups. Group 1 will find several passages that support the idea that salvation is a spiritual phenomenon and emphasizes eternal life. Group 2 will find passages that support the idea that salvation consists of physical healing, relief, and service. Come together to share what you find. Then decide together which definition of salvation Jesus seems to support the most?

Talk together about how you would combine the two views of salvation to form a program for salvation for Christians today.

Option C: Notice the relationship between Jesus and synagogue officials in the passage for this session. Also note any references to chief priests or Pharisees in Mark 2:23-28; 7:1-7; and 15:30-31. Why do you think religious leaders reacted the way they did to Jesus when he healed people physically? How do religious leaders today respond to occasions of physical healing? How do religious leaders today regard physical well-being as opposed to spiritual well-being?

Respond (15 MINUTES)

Option A: Brainstorm an evangelism program for your congregation that attends to both the physical health and the spiritual health of people. Then brainstorm a service program for your congregation that incorporates a component of salvation into acts of service. What would these two programs look like? Is it possible to be the church of Christ with only one of these programs? If so, which is more important? Why?

Option B: Share stories about how an experience of physical salvation changed you or someone you know. Tell how salvation or healing changed and deepened your relationship with God. Then talk as a group about how much convincing people need to change their lives? Should we be able to be faithful with fewer miracles and acts of salvation? When is it too late in life to change and be saved? Is it possible to be saved eternally, if we've never experienced God's saving acts in this life?

Closing (5 MINUTES)

Gather in a circle. Pray silently for understanding of the relationship between physical and spiritual salvation. Close by singing a prayer song of healing, such as "There is a balm in Gilead" or "My life flows on."

Part III: Leader Guidelines

Tips for Leading

1. Try an object lesson to demonstrate the relationship between physical and spiritual salvation. Show objects that have two parts, both parts being essential to the proper work or use of the object, such as a hammer (handle and head).
2. Make people feel comfortable with differences in belief about salvation. The notion of salvation as a physical phenomenon in the New Testament may be controversial. Encourage each person to speak his or her mind without condemning the beliefs of others. Assure people that both views of salvation are present in the Bible and are not exclusive of one anther.
3. As you study the Bible text together, keep reviewing the views of salvation studied in earlier sessions, relating them to the definition of salvation in this session. Reinforce the notion that salvation is not a simple, one-dimensional concept in scripture.

Session 5
Salvation as Conversion and Calling

Part I: Preparation

Bible Passage: Galatians 1:13–2:10

Key verses: But when God, who had set me apart before I was born and called me through his grace, was pleased to reveal his Son to me, so that I might proclaim him among the Gentiles (Gal. 1:15-16b).

Summary: Paul tells his life's story in Galatians 1:13–2:10, at least one version of it. He tells that God had a plan for him from before his birth, which included his Jewish upbringing, his conversion to Christianity, and his ministry to Gentiles. This story enlarges on the common story of Paul's conversion found in Acts 9 where God comes to Paul in mid-life and converts him to faith in a dramatic way. Whether by proper upbringing or spectacular lightening bolts, Paul is saved by the grace of God. But for what purpose does God save Paul or any one of us? Paul does not merely rest on the fact that he is saved. He responds with a ministry to serve God. Does God require a response from everyone? Is everyone called to serve? Is salvation truly salvation if we don't respond to God's great gift?

Study

In Galatians, Paul gives us a version of his autobiography, a personal account of his life in which he claims God set him apart from before his birth for a mission to defend the gospel to Gentiles. Having lived at the time of Jesus and the disciples, but having never served Christ directly, Paul was not considered one of the original apostles. However, by demonstrating that he was part of God's plan all along to carry the gospel to the Gentiles, he was defending his apostleship to the Galatians.

Salvation as Conversion and Calling

Paul begins the story of his life before he became a Christian and recounts significant events up until the end of the Jerusalem conference reported in Acts 15. At least on the surface this seems to be the case. However, matching Paul's account of his life in Galatians with the account of his ministry in Acts is a difficult proposition. In the end, however, the way in which Paul is saved and converted is less important than the fact that this persecutor of Christians was embraced by God and given an important task to do—to serve God.

The autobiography of Paul in Galatians also serves as a prologue to his confrontation with Peter in Antioch. With this confrontation over ministry to Gentiles, Paul and Peter go their separate ways. Paul travels west and to the Gentile world, while Peter remains the apostle in the East. This may seem strange since Peter is the first one to have extended the offer of the gospel to a Gentile (Acts 10). But the wide differences between the two are useful in pointing up the variety of ways people are converted to faith and the variety of ways they perform Christian service as a response to God's gift of salvation.

> The most frequent term for Christian people in Paul's writings is "called to be saints." It seems that to be a Christian is to be called. A problem today is that so many Christians seem to lack a sense of calling.

While gratitude and inner peace are always appropriate responses to salvation, Paul carries the banner for the idea that Christians are saved to serve, or to use Paul's own terms, we have been reconciled to God so that we might become God's agents of reconciliation (2 Cor. 5:18-21). The ministry that Paul wages, giving his whole life to establish churches in Gentile territory, is in proportion to his spectacular experience of God's salvation. Every offer of salvation is a powerful one that requires a powerful response from the saved.

Paul defines his experience of salvation as a "calling" rather than a "conversion," something more than a sudden change in belief. A study Bible with annotations will indicate that Paul's calling is similar in this regard to Jeremiah's calling in Jeremiah 1:4-10, where God has a plan of action for those who are saved. Read the words of the prophet and note how both Jeremiah and Paul were consecrated from the womb, that is, before birth, and set apart for service to God. Also compare the way Paul speaks of revelation, claiming that his message was not from men, not even from the Jerusalem apostles, but from God, to the way God put words in the mouth of Jeremiah. Both are appointed as messengers, apostles to "the nations," that is, the Gentiles.

Conversion has become a static term for what happens when one becomes a Christian. In some respect we believe that because we are saved we can sit back and relax! We often think that what needed to happen has happened in a spiritual moment and now we can get on with life. To see salvation as a calling, however, is to acknowledge that salvation is dynamic. We are called *to* something, to be engaged in a process, in a task, in a mission. We are reconciled so we can serve. No longer is it life as usual, because we are no longer the same.

> Conversion is the quick fix for what ails you. Calling is God's long-term therapy for your life.

So why do we put so much emphasis on the dramatic account of Paul's conversion as told in Acts 9, instead of his less dramatic but perhaps more important calling? Perhaps because it makes more interesting reading. Read Acts 9 and then Galatians 1:13–2:10 to see how Paul broadens and deepens his salvation story in the latter. Then reread Acts 9 with the knowledge that God is saving Paul in whatever way for some purpose, some response, some ministry. Look for the sense of calling that is also present in the dramatic story in Acts 9.

Whether by blinding light or gentle upbringing, salvation happens in more than one way. And having been saved, our responses to God's gift are varied as well. The Hebrews responded by worshiping God. Jeremiah responded by speaking the truth to God's people. Peter responded by proclaiming Jesus to the Jews. And Paul responded by taking the gospel to the Gentiles. However we experience God's miraculous gift of salvation, we too have a calling to serve God. Our response will turn us from believers into doers of the word, from believers to disciples, from believers to apostles for the gospel.

Things to think about: Talk to a person this week who experienced salvation as a lightening bolt experience. Also talk to a person who is saved, but who cannot point to the hour and the day of conversion. Find out how the experience of salvation changed them. What kind of "calling" does each have? That is, how has each responded to the gift of salvation?

Consider your own calling. Are you an underachiever or an overachiever when it comes to serving God? What could you do in your church, your community, or elsewhere to serve God more?

Salvation as Conversion and Calling

Part II: Session

Focus (10 minutes)
Gather for announcements and sharing. Then choose one of the following exercises to focus on the topic.

Option A: Learning life's lessons. When did you have to be struck by a lightening bolt to learn a lesson in life about the opposite sex, cars, school, parents, children, money, or other tough problems? Decide who in the group has the most dramatic lightening bolt story. Award that person an imaginary diploma from the School of Hard Knocks. Then talk generally about how you personally learn lessons in life. Are you able to learn from other's mistakes? from the advice of others? from the experience of others, such as parents and teachers? from your own mistakes?

> Just as there is no real belief without commitment, so there is no true love without expression.

Option B: Pick a point. On a continuum between an experience of being nurtured in faith throughout your life and an experience of sudden conversion, where would you place yourself? Form a human continuum along an imaginary line across the room, or draw a line on newsprint and label the extreme ends call and conversion. Take turns putting a dot on the line at the place that represents your personal experience. Were you converted at a very definite moment? Or did you grow up in faith, never really doubting. As a group, stand back and look at the arrangement of dots on the continuum. Describe any patterns or trends you see.

Transition: The Apostle Paul's dramatic conversion on the road to Damascus is famous. So viciously opposed to Christianity was Paul that it took blinding lights and the voice of God to make him see the truth. Paul himself, however, testifies that even before this experience, God saved Paul and laid claim on him for a ministry to the Gentiles. Compare Paul's salvation stories to see the variety of ways God saves.

Engage the Text (20 minutes)
Option A: See the different sides of Paul. Divide into two groups of two or more people. Group 1 will look at Acts 9. Group 2 will look at Galatians 1:13–2:10. If you have enough people for a third group, Group 3 will look at Jeremiah 1:4-10. In each group, list the ways Paul's or Jeremiah's life changed as a result of God's hand upon him. Come back together to compare lists. How are the responses to God's call similar or different? Would

you say that one method of salvation in the Bible is better than another? Which one? Why? Which, if any, does Paul believe is more authentic?

Option B: Look at conversion and call stories throughout the Bible. Individually or in groups of two or three people, choose a name and scripture text from the following list.

Naaman (2 Kings 5)
Samuel (1 Sam. 1:9-28)
David (1 Sam. 16:1-13)
Nathanael (John 1:43-51),
Zacchaeus (Luke 19:1-10)
Samaritan woman (John 4:1-30)
Isaiah (Isa. 6)
Ruth (Ruth 1:1-18)

Answer the following questions regarding the Bible character you chose.
1. How did this person come to faith?
2. Was this person's salvation a conversion or a calling?
3. What did God call this person to do?

Come back together to present your Bible character and your group responses to the questions.

Respond (15 MINUTES)
Option A: Find your calling: If salvation includes your response to God's gift, think about what God is calling you to do or be. Take turns completing the sentence that begins: "Since I've become a Christian, I feel called to…"

Option B: Identify a calling in others. Sometimes it is easier to see how God intends to use others than it is to see our own calling. And when others recognize an ability in you, they authenticate what you might feel to be true. As a group, concentrate on each person individually, naming aloud the calling you see in that person. If you prefer, write a sentence about each person on individual slips of paper and deliver your sentences to the others in the group. Take time to read the slips you receive, offering them out loud if you wish.

Salvation as Conversion and Calling

Option C: Choose topics for discussion. As a group, talk about one or more of the following issues as time allows.
1. Can a person be truly saved if he or she does not turn to serve God in some way?
2. What is a sufficient response to God's call upon our lives?
3. What is an authentic salvation experience?
4. If a person does not confess faith in this life, will God still save him or her? Will God save people who confess faith at the very end of life?
5. What is the earliest age at which a person is truly able to respond to God's gift of salvation?
6. What are the signs of maturity that indicate a person is able to join in a relationship with God?

Closing (5 MINUTES)
Gather in a circle. From an attitude of silent prayer, name aloud some of the ways your congregation has responded to the gift of salvation that God gives. Offer these responses up to God as a gift. End the prayer with the Lord's Prayer.

PART III: LEADER GUIDELINES

Tips for Leading
1. Urge people to speak openly and honestly of their conversion experience or experiences. People find it difficult to talk about these inner, very private, and personal matters. To encourage people to speak, agree together that the information shared in this setting is confidential.
2. Participants may have very definite beliefs about conversion. Avoid two things: efforts to change someone's mind and efforts to discount the beliefs of people who believe differently from most.
3. To allow more people to share in each exercise, consider breaking into small groups. Remain together as one group if facilities or acoustics don't warrant small groups. In large groups, encourage frequent contributors to wait until others have spoken before entering the conversation. Consider contacting a variety of people in the group beforehand to be thinking of their conversion experience. Then call on them during the session to get the conversation going.

Session 6
Saved by Grace, Judged by Works

Part I: Preparation

Bible Passage: Romans 2:1–3:31

Key verses: For God shows no partiality. All who have sinned apart from the law will also perish apart from the law, and all who have sinned under the law will be judged by the law. For it is not the hearers of the law who are righteous in God's sight, but the doers of the law who will be justified (Rom. 2:11-13).

Summary: Paul's name is synonymous with salvation by grace. He devoted much of his ministry to refuting the idea that people can earn their salvation by being good and keeping religious laws. But in these chapters in Romans, Paul argues powerfully for doing good works. He drives home the point in this passage that God's gift of salvation neither frees us from God's judgment nor gives us the right to judge others. Is Paul changing his mind? If our relationship with God in salvation does not preserve us from judgment, if it does not find us innocent, why should we want to be saved?

Study

Judged by the law? Can this be Paul speaking? What ever happened to justification by faith? Since when will we be judged by how well or how poorly we keep the law?

In this section of Romans, Paul is turning his attention from his main ministry to Gentiles to speaking to Christians in Rome, some of whom are Jews and some Gentiles. There is an ongoing discussion between the two groups over who is an authentic Christian. What is significant for us

Saved by Grace, Judged by Works

> For truly I tell you, until heaven and earth pass away, not one letter, not one stroke of a letter, will pass from the law until all is accomplished.
>
> —Matthew 5:18

in our study of salvation is that Paul does not sound here like Paul as he talks to the old guard, Jewish Christians. Or at least he is not speaking like the Paul that we usually think of in the Bible. In this passage he does not claim, as he does so many times, that the law is null and void. In fact, the law helps Christians to be faithful. While all will be saved by grace, all will be judged by the same criterion—*according to their works*. In other words, it's not *having* the law in our pedigree, but doing it that counts. It's not only having faith that's important, but being faithful. All will be judged by the same standard; the ones who do the law will be justified.

On the one hand, it sounds as if Paul is vindicating the Jews. In these chapters he clearly holds up the law that has been so central to the Jewish faith. In fact, Paul vindicates the law itself and not the people. He cautions the Jews about believing that because they keep the commandments, they may judge others.

Paul's arguments are not all that strange. Look at some of the verses that illustrate his reasoning. This section of Romans ends at 3:31 with a rhetorical question, a question whose answer we already know. Do we then overthrow the law by this faith? By no means! On the contrary, we uphold the law. Paul wants to stress that his teaching about the law of faith is not intended to contradict it; to the contrary, his teaching upholds the law and puts it on a firmer foundation. Also, in 2:17-29 Paul puts a great emphasis on *doing*. The true Jew is not the one who is circumcised according to the law, but the one who does what the laws call for, and a Gentile who follows the law therefore has a circumcision of the heart. For each group of Christians, it is not the outward sign of circumcision, but the dedication to living the commandments that is important. Again the emphasis is not on having something but on doing something.

By the time we come to Romans 3:20-24, we recognize the familiar Paul again. These are verses many Christians know by heart and quote often because they express the essence of the gospel as faith rather than works. So how do we put the two Pauls together, the one who calls for works and the one who criticizes good works? One way is to understand that Paul is speaking in different contexts or to people in different stages of the new Christian experience.

To the Jews, who had lived strictly according to the law, Paul makes a corrective saying that we join God's club through faith alone. We cannot force entry by our own works. To the Gentiles, who have experienced a life of faith but not the disciplined life of the commandments, Paul makes another corrective, emphasizing the importance of living a good and righteous life alongside believing. He warns all Christians, Gentile and Jewish, that salvation by faith is no cause to be overconfident about God's favor. God shows no partiality to the saved and expects each one to strive for righteousness and obedience.

There are some very typical things about Paul in this passage. Everyone is equal: Gentile and Jew, slave and free, male and female. We are especially equal as sinners. By virtue of being human, we are sinners even if we're saved. The only thing that distinguishes us are our efforts to do the good thing. Therefore, everyone will be judged according to their works. As one scholar puts it, *Saved by faith, judged by works.* Faith and works are not opposites, but are different parts of a whole. They are the answers to different questions. Faith answers the question, How do I get into the fellowship of God's people? Works answers the question, How do I maintain membership in this fellowship?

> Do not be deceived; God is not mocked, for you reap whatever you sow.
> —Galatians 6:7

So if salvation does not afford us the sensation that we've made it, that we're safe, that we can stop striving, why do we bother? Couldn't we just wait until the end of life, live the way we wish and convert near the end of life? As Paul would say, "By no means!" The law is not the way *to* salvation but it is the way *of* salvation. Having been justified and reconciled to God, the commandments guide us in the way of life in Christ. That leaves us with our final rhetorical question: who wouldn't want to live a life that brings the greatest joy, now and always?

PART II: SESSION

Focus (10 MINUTES)
Gather for announcements and sharing before delving into the Bible study. Then choose one of the exercises below to focus on the topic.

Option A: Talk your way out of trouble. Appoint people in the group to talk their way out of the following situations by arguing they are above criticism.

1. You are a speeder. Convince a police officer that you have been approved for a license and therefore don't need to be disciplined by an officer.
2. You are an Academy Award winning actor who gets a bad review in the newspaper for a performance. Defend your reputation.
3. You are a congregation that advocates environmental stewardship based on the Bible, but you use Styrofoam at church potlucks. How do you explain this hypocrisy?

Transition: Sometimes we think our salvation makes us special in God's eyes. Then it follows that the better we are, the more qualified we are to judge others and the more immune we are to criticism. This is the attitude that Paul addresses in Romans 2–3. It leads him to say some interesting things about religious law and salvation.

Option B: Talk about how each of the following could be a parable for salvation by grace. Also talk about the responsibilities that come with each.
- Winning one million dollars in the lottery
- Love at first sight
- Perfect pitch
- Miraculous recovery from a terminal illness

Transition: While Paul preached over and over again that there is nothing we can do to earn salvation, he never said that the free gift of salvation made us immune to God's judgment. Turn to Romans 2–3 to find out how salvation changes things.

Engage the Text (20 MINUTES)

Option A: Listen to Paul from two vantage points. First look together at the introduction to Romans in a study Bible. Read about the Christians to whom Paul is speaking in Romans 12:1-3. Make a list of characteristics. Then put yourself in the shoes of someone who is as yet unconverted. Listen and follow along in a Bible as a volunteer reads Romans 2:1-11. How do you think the unconverted would understand the conversion process from this passage? Then put yourself in the shoes of someone who is already a confessing Christian. Listen as the passage is read again. How does the message change for you?

Option B: Get a better understanding of what God expects from the faithful. Listen as someone reads Romans 12. Then discuss the following questions.

1. Name ways that we are sinners and "fall short of the glory of God" (Rom. 3:23).
2. How can we be sinners and do the will of God at the same time?
3. How much of this list of good works is actually doable? To what extent does God expect too much?
4. When does God judge us? At the time we confess our faith? At the end of life? Both?
5. After reading Romans 2–3, do you think God will judge the faithful more generously or more severely than the unfaithful? Why?

Option C: Nobody got it right. Not the Gentiles nor the Jews. Divide into two groups, one to look at Jewish Christians and one to look at Gentile Christians. The Jewish group will read Romans 2:17-29. The Gentile group will read 1 Corinthians 1.

In both groups, discuss the following questions and appoint someone in the group to report back to the larger group.
1. According to the passage you read, what were Jews emphasizing in their Christian faith? What were Gentiles emphasizing in their Christian faith?
2. What happens when the Jews pride themselves on keeping the commandments? What happens when the Gentiles pride themselves on their newfound faith just because they believe?
3. What problem does your group have with the other group? Why can or can't you get along?
4. What was the danger your group encountered by emphasizing only one angle of Christian faith?
5. What does Paul want your group to do to balance faith and law? (Gentiles, look quickly through all of 1 Corinthians for ideas).

Come back together as a whole group and listen to the reports of both groups.

Respond (15 MINUTES)
Option A: Keep your membership current. We have seen in this series of lessons that salvation in the Bible has several dimensions, physical and spiritual, present and future, passive and active. This lesson has focused on the active dimension. Take stock of your Christian life.
1. Have you experienced God's love and calling?
2. What is your calling?
3. Have you committed yourself to this calling?
4. How do you keep your batteries charged and your mind renewed?

5. What are your active dimensions?
6. What are or might be your growing edges?

Option B: What do you have to say for yourself? Imagine that you will die tomorrow and will face God's judgment. Write a defense of your life showing that you lived the way of salvation. If you are willing, share your defense with the group. Or if you'd rather, write your confession, listing the ways you fell short of God's glory. Talk generally about people's reliance on God's mercy. Do we rely on it too much or too little? Why?

Closing (5 MINUTES)

Listen as someone reads 1 Corinthians 13 aloud. Close with sentence prayers committing yourselves to live out your faith in love of God and others.

PART III: LEADER GUIDELINES

Tips for Leading

1. This lesson brings the series on salvation to a close. Save a little time at the end of the session to evaluate the unit. Talk together about what new insights people gained. How was their thinking changed or reinforced? What questions do people still have?
2. At the heart of this lesson is the relationship between salvation and obedience. Help the class understand that salvation is God's work, but obedience is our work in response to God's grace.
3. If it is appropriate in the discussion of God's judgment, talk together about guilt. Help people think of guilt not as a millstone, but as a great motivator for change and reconciliation. Encourage people to get rid of guilt by making a change in their faith lives.